# KENERLY PRESENTS

## LASHAI WC

KENERLY PRESENTS

LASHAI WOOD

Printed in the United States of America

Paperback Version:

ISBN-13: 978-0615764870

ISBN-10: 0615764878

Kenerly Presents in association with AMB
Publishing Productions

shauntakenerly@yahoo.com

KENERLY PRESENTS

LASHAI WOOD

# BETWEEN THE SHEETS

## BY LASHAI WOOD

# ACKNOWLEDGEMENTS

First and foremost, I thank the Lord
God, my Savior, for his mercy and
grace
for the day that HE has made
and for the Gifts of Shades of Shai
My seeds, "My I's" Irving and I'esha,
for giving me a reason to live and for
teaching me how to love,
the only two things that can NEVER
be taken away from me
now dats wassup
My mother and father Frances and
Herbert Lee
for creating me
and my entire FAMILY
for loving and accepting my good,
my bad, and my ugly
Don't know what I would do without
my BIG's,
Angie, Dray, and Ms. Brig
for always giving me something to
look up to, even growing up as kids

Azikiwe, for being my ROCK and my
definition of Faith
My substance of things HOPED for
my LOVE, my best friend,
and so much more
I thank my tight circle that keeps me
going and growing,
Meco, Qwin, Mike (PinkToe),
Donnie, Nook, my ride or die chick,
Celiar, my Pineapple, and Pickaway
Peeps
my girl Crystal for putting the first
mic in my hand and setting my stage
for me to expand.
I'm so in love with our vibe.
Last, but definitely not least, I thank
Shaunta Kenerly and
AMB Publishing
for believing in me and giving me this
opportunity to be heard.

L.O.E
Loyalty Over Everything

KENERLY PRESENTS

LASHAI WOOD

# TABLE OF CONTENTS

KENERLY PRESENTS
LASHAI WOOD

*Signs*

*With You*

*One Or The Other*

*Do It Again*

*Bust-A-Move*

*Love Is Great*

*A Place I Call Home*

*Home*

*It Shouldn't Matter*

*Now Hear This*

*Feel So Good*

*I Like*

*Rapper's Delight*

*This or That*

*Drinks on Me*

*Peace*

*I Miss You*

*U Might Be But It Still Ain't Me*

*Why I Chose To Love*

*My Dad Say*

*Sista 2 Sista*

*Cash Ova Everythang*

*Love Don't Cost A Thing*

*Whenever I Want 2*

*It's Like Candy*

*I'm Hungry*

*SMDH*

*A Letter from my Love*

# INTRODUCTION

Utilize my expressions and escape
into my lyrical café'
don't worry bout getting drunk,
the drinks are on me
hoping your drunkenness will help
you see things my way
Bold stories and deep feelings that
must be exposed
I'm pouring sensation deep into your
soul
It's sorta like healing, if you will
I'm giving you something you can
feel
It's not just the way I say things,
it's what all I have to say
my deepest thoughts brought to you
by SHADES OF SHAI…
These are not just individual poems
but if you read in between the lines
and in its entirety
I just invited thee
to explore my hidden stories

# BETWEEN THE SHEETS
where the paper and my pen meets
and becomes lover and friends
over and over again.......

### *Between the sheets,*
is where our bodies meet
I'm 41 Hot and at my sexual peak
happily divorced so I no longer have
to creep
he fresh out da joint so his shit he no
longer have to beat
which means no more masturbating
for me
He's got me wide open so he can
enter deep
and I will please him from his head all
the way down to his feet
His pants is packed so I've found the
beef
my body is buffet style open all night
so it's all he can eat
he down for whatever just to please
me
don't wanna toot my own horn but
beep beep
my good loving is all he wants and
needs
and his cravings is what I seek

Appetites totally satisfied now we off
to sleep
cuddling up close in
BETWEEN THE SHEETS

# DIDN'T CHA KNOW?

Allow me to take you inside the mind
of dis real Bitch
don't wanna call it a vacation,
but let's take a trip
so follow the directions
Map Quest to perfection
keep yo eyes on the road and listen to
directions
Slow down nigga, is you deaf?
I said make a right, not left
or you gon get left behind
not at a red-light, but at the stop sign
meaning NO traffic
shady communication makes traveling
havoc
Didn't cha know, I'm one-way Shai
and I'm not having it
You not leaving me out here to get
lost
when you and I both know this
road is blocked off

I know which way I'm suppose to go
don't like being stuck in a one lane
without no traffic flow
put yo metal to the pedal,
cause
dis Bitch gots-to-go
life is too short or
DIDN'T CHA KNOW?

# B.I.T.C.H.

There's more to being a *B.I.T.C.H.*
other than the way it flows from yo
lips
U see *B.I.T.C.Hes* are Beautiful,
Intelligent,
Talented, Courageous, Hero's
and if U don't know, now U know,
so…


Get hungry *B.I.T.C.H.*
Stay on the grind and shit
Don't live for another expectations of
U
stay hustling, grinding doing whatever
U need to do
just for U, so what that nigga don't
do, won't do,
it's cool, makes it easier to recognize
good brothas that do
See beyond what's in front of U
there is a bigger picture,
force and demand a better future
Instead of waiting and contemplating

about a situation, without hesitation
know exactly what needs to be done
be confident, knowing that U are the
one

Stay hungry, stay focused *B.I.T.C.H.*
Stand for something, stop falling for
all this dumb shit
Acquiring more on your own, for your
own, creates less stress
and having to deal with a bunch of
mess, there's fewer test
Cherish that pussy, it's God's gift, that
shit is priceless
instead of giving it away like
government cheese, *B.I.T.C.H.* please

Getting all mad and wondering why
they call U a *Bitch*, in the bad sense
Well, *Bitch* U allow them to, dancing
to this bullshit us real women would
call abuse
Verbally stripping U of the
self-respect that your presence should
demand

yet U walk around here wit yo video
clothes on trying to impress this man,
that man, any man sitting next to the
man, sitting next to the got damn man
physically doing all U can to get some
holla
but if U selling yoself cheap *Bitch*,
why even bother

Stay on the grind, don't get left
behind, educate yo mind
stop wasting precious time, press fast-
forward not rewind
so that the next time
U are faced with adversity and shit
pop yo collar, cause U are a
*B.I.T.C.H.*
A Beautiful, Intelligent, Talented,
Courageous, Hero
and if U don't know, now U know
*B.I.T.C.H.*

# CELL PHONE JONES

My cell phone jones makes me wanna

SPRINT to you

and bend dis NEXTEL over like

doggies do

text me and make my T-MOBILE

vibrate Boo

I just wanna feel your VERIZON beat

up my CRICKET

but not too fast, don't wanna use up

all yo daytime minutes

Don't worry bout me, my shits

unlimited

so please take more than a minute

You see we can get-it-in on yo free

nights and weekends

just lock my number in,

THEN you can BOOST up these

thighs

and chirp it on the side

then roam, roam, roam

please baby, baby, please pick-up yo
cell phone

KENERLY PRESENTS

LASHAI WOOD

# R&B

I'm feelin' real R&B,
as the smooth groves move,
hypnotize and sex me
with its harmony

D'Angelo got me "cruising" but I'm
feelin' Smokey
head rocking, body relaxing while

Dr. Dre's "chronic" choke me

If "u-n-i-t-y" is all we need
then why in the hell haven't Jahiem
got wit me?
Now I know he aint no Teddy P
But he still can close the door and
"come on and go with me"

Cause Jamie's got me feelin' Foxxy
with my
"T-shirt and panties" on
Got played by Cisco because I didn't
have no "thong song"

But I'm feelin' real R&B,
as the smooth groves move,
hypnotize and sex me
with its harmony

Teddy Riley can go "deep, deep,
deep"
soooooooo deep, using Silk to get me
"freaky"
R. Kelley is on the phone cause his
"body's calling for me"

Now everything will be alright
as long as at 10 till Brain McKnight
"You give me love, love, love, love
crazy love"
It's not that hard Donell, stop Jonesin'
"You know what's up"

Just promise to be "forever mine"
like the O'Jays
or something like Jodeci
"and baby won't you please stay
for a little while"

Cause I'm feelin' real R&B,

as the smooth groves move,
hypnotize and sex me
with its harmony
It beats passion in me
Now that's what I call R&B

# UNCONDITIONALLY MINE

Unconditionally mine
forever withstanding the test of time
Our friendship has always been so
mental and confidential
for reasons that we both agree
but whenever in need
you've always been there for me
No matter what's at stake
you've always done whatever it takes
offering solutions to my mistakes
relieving heartaches without getting
all physical with me
keeping the vibe we share, friendly
I love the way you express your
admirations for me
simply by being a true friend
displaying characteristics of a real
man.
Something so rare and so hard to find
someone like you who's
unconditionally mine....

# IF...

IF is a mighty BIG word,
IF you capitalize the I
IF you could make it happen, then
why ask why?
anything is possible,
IF you're willing to try
IF you were a piece of candy,
you'd be chocolaty-smooth
something served before sex with
strawberries, to get me in the mood
IF you were a beverage, you'd be a
double shot of Hennessey
Stiff, dark liquor with no ice, just
what my mouth, throat, and body
needs
IF you were something to eat, you'd
be my favorite piece of cake
yellow with butter-cream icing
cumming towards my face
IF you were the weather, you'd be a
sunny-rainy day
your presence shines and brings a
smile to my face

your quiet storm makes me wet all
over the place
your arms would be my shelter and
my escape
If you were a mattress, you'd be
king-size
high enough that I'd have to jump on
top of to get inside
cold until I get under yo sheets
gets so warm when our body's roll
around in dem sheets
gets even hotter when our bodies
freak
If you were an article of clothing,
you'd be my favorite pair of boxers,
loose fitting
easy access for getting
what's in dem draws
complemented by a wife-beater with
no bra
enticed by the harden nipples that you
saw
ready, willing, and able at my every
beckon call

If you were an instrument, you'd be a
Saxophone
yo sexy sounds would make me sway,
close my eyes and moan
and make me wanna get it on and on
I would love for you to blow sweet
melodies slow
making my body respond to your
harmonious flow
allowing your rhythm to reach out and
touch my soul
my heartbeat is yours to have and to
hold
IF tomorrow were not promised,
would you waste precious time away?
Well tomorrows not promised, so stop
putting off what you can do today…

# HE'S CEREAL

Cause he's ce-real
something like milky with a sugary
feel
topped with banana without the peel

As I lay in my lil' niggas arms
I could feel his Lucky Charms
He makes me coo-coo for Cocoa
Puffs
he's the Captain of my Crunch

His Apple Jacks all Rice and Krispie
POP<CRACKLE<SNAP
get-it, from the back
um yall aint ready for dat

His Honey Nut Cheerios and my
Honey Combs
produced Frosted Flakes
and Fruity Pebbles all over the place

Cause he's ce-real
something like milky with a sugary
feel
topped with banana without the peel

I like his Trix, oh that silly rabbit
his Cinnamon Toast Crunch I just
gotta have it
he makes my Cookie Crisp
Fruity Loops is how our tongues kiss

Oh I'm getting too excited, let me
stop
but I can't even fight it, I just gotta
have my POPS!!

Cause he's ce-real
something like milky with a sugary
feel
topped with banana without the peel

*HE'S CEREAL*

# HIS KISS

When I lick my lips, umm
I can still taste HIS KISS
his thickness, his chocolate, all up in
this
exploring my Atlantic Ocean
traveling slow then fast, then in
circular motions
His lips, his tongue, so thick and
sweet
our mouths together is such a
delicious treat
the heat from his mouth warms my
entire soul
with just one kiss I lose control as my
body explodes
sending me on an exotic ride
contracting my walls pulling him
deeper inside
and hell naw, you can't have
none of this
I'm his temple, these are his lips, just
for his dick,

only for HIS KISS
So while you're out there doing all
that kissing and shit
remember this, choose wisely
because you don't have to share
HIS KISS…

# MY HUSBAND

I get breakfast in bed, toes sucked,
and dick fed
by the same man day in and day out
I'm down with O.D.D. now dats what
I'm talking bout
One Damn Dick supplying me
one man's needs to fulfill,
exclusive ecstasy
and when he touches my skin,
it feels like he's caressing my insides
my body and soul replies
Wet soft kisses tingles my spirit
his reassurance allows me to love
freely and not fear it
Needing his heart to complete me
his commitment and our marriage
stamps a lifetime guarantee
finding strength and determination in
our unity
sprinkled by God's grace,
which opens our hearts and eyes to
see
And when it comes to he and me

33

we fit together like jigsaw puzzles do
regardless of what, when, where, or
who
I wouldn't want to live without a love
so true
I'm crazy about this man,
I'm his number one fan
I'm his wife and he is
MY HUSBAND…

# MAKING LOVE

The sound of your voice
makes me moist
after a night of complete ecstasy
I know you was on top, we kissed, I
looked into your eyes
but I could of swore you were inside
of me
literally, the way you dug around in
My Lady
a-construction-worker-in-yo-pass-life,
you had to be
or a wrestler, the way you be WWFn'
me
sexually freeing me
giving my mind and body all they
need
Your thirst for me
I'll quench
with the juices my body produces as I
pinch
every inch of you

causing my body's nectar to explode
like the lava from volcanoes do
my body loves tasting and making
love to you….

# THERE'S NOTHING LIKE THIS

There's nothing like the feel of a
man's touch
especially when that man is yours
There's nothing more precious
than feeling adored
There's nothing like the feeling of
"This is all you've prayed for"
There's nothing like making love
to the one you're in love with
There's nothing like smooches
that tingles like your very first kiss
There's nothing like showing God
just how grateful you are
There's nothing like getting there
after you've traveled so far
And let me be the first to admit
there is nothing, I mean
Nothing Like This…

# TRIPPIN'

Insecurity is a trip
and although I consider myself pretty
confident
there are moments I wonder where his
time is spent

I get an attitude, my mind be playing
tricks on me
be feeling uptight
some of our best days, be feeling like
our worst nights
sometimes confronted by thoughts of
if he's doing me right

Why would he withhold his lovin'
from me
hide his feeling inside, afraid to let his
heart free
why can't he see that growth is what
we need
I feel empty wondering if he's into me

Where is the desire, the fire
burning passion that's supposed to
heat my soul
When I ask for some, he play dumb
like he don't even know
when we make love is the only time it
really shows
other than that, I'm lonely and that
really blows

I'm scared because I know these
mixed emotions
can lead to double dippin'
I hope we fix this soon before I gets to
trippin'

# LOVE IS NOT BLIND

I don't like being taken for granted
or you having a sista feeling slanted
Got me bent like whoa,
feeling like hell-to-the-no
I don't deserve this shit
especially when I don't ask for much
and I'm a 24-7, ride or die Bitch
down for whatever and shit
and all I want is just a little bit
and you got the nerve to trip
when you the one not giving your all
up in this bitch
and I got all-of-dis loving that is
priceless
Show me you love me
throw me like you know me,
nigga you owe me
this aint the way it's supposed to be

I'm yours and you are all mine,
you got me feeling like I'm on
borrowed time
neglecting me is a gotdamn crime
I know we both wear glasses but love
is not blind….

# WHAT IS LOVE???

What is love without honesty
What is love without the O or the E
What is love if your heart can't be
freed
What is love if it can't be found
within
What is love if we're just lovers and
not friends
What if you didn't know that GOD is
where true love begins….

# WHEN A SISTA GON GET SOME ACT-RIGHT??

I swear I love being married but at
times I really miss being yo woman,
when we use to fuck, fuck, fuck, fuck,
fuck, for little or nothing
Now we make love sweet love,
whenever we can
I'm not complaining I'm just saying
how easy it is to forget those little
things
romance, dating, hello and goodbye
kisses
compliments, sexy voice messages
afternoon phone calls just to say,
I love you
Smiling and day-dreaming about last
night,

with visions of how you love me right


Loving me more than just paying the
bills
sprinkle me with some passion,
Envogue me, give me something I can
feel a Let me try to make this
perfectly clear, you must have and to
hold me
don't cheat me but keep me, respect
and try to satisfy me completely
emotionally, mentally, and especially
physically
don't forget the spirit that's growing
inside of me
I hope it's not intentional but I gotta
let you know
Baby you've gotten just a little too
comfortable
and because I love you with all my
might
I just have one question
When a sista gon get some act-right??

# I'M YOUR WIFE

Words can hurt no matter what they
say
looks can abuse in the same damn
way
Sometimes I need to be heard and not
spoken to
allow me to have feelings without
having to justify them to you
I don't come to you, for you to make
me feel worst
so watch your tone and kill the
sarcastic outburst
Please let me express myself
I want to find comfort in you and
nobody else
I'd rather hurt with you than hurt by
my damn self
I'd rather be healed by you than
anyone else

Fuck a rebound
no matter how desperate I might
sound

I wanna be down
with you, Boo
I want to get this shit right
what we share is supposed to be one
love and one life
I'm not your girl anymore
damn-it
I'm your wife….

# KENERLY PRESENTS
## LASHAI WOOD

# GIT-R-DONE

It's real cold in here and I'm not
talking about the A/C
naw nigga, your emotions and
affection is on 20 degrees
and with the wind chill factor,
it feels more like zero below
yet you walk around here freezing
like you don't know
it's cold
You still don't know how to treat me
almost clueless on how to keep me
but how can that be,
when I'm telling you constantly
what I need
When will our situation change?
If never, then how long can I play this
game?
Or continue to lose, because losing is
something I don't like to do
but in loving you, losing is something
I've gotten use to
But I can't take this shit no more,

It's time to even the score
being alone feels no better than being
left alone
what's the point of living together and
you're not happy at home
it's sad that you still haven't learned,
just where I'm coming from
I feel like it's up to you to fix what
we've begun
So roll up your sleeves,
and
Git-R-Done….

# WHAT'S GOING ON?

You say I'm never happy, I say you
treat me crappy
and this shits been going on for far
too long
Tell me, what's going on?

I miss you so much and you live right
here
I be needing to feel your touch but
you won't cum here
Sleeping next to you night after night
with your back to me
all night my body aching for some
touchy feely
and when I try to get close, you're
either too tired, drunk, or sleepy
seem like we fuck weekly
Tell me, what's going on?

Your need to be away from home, all
day, without picking up the phone

to me, that is dead wrong
you need to spend more time at home
I feel like a kid visiting on the
weekends
not even lovers something like
friends
Away is how your time is spent
weeks go by before you give me the
business
I'm starting to wonder if you even
miss this
When was the last time we really
hugged or our tongue kissed
I would like them more than just
when we have sex
Tell me, what's going on?

How is it that we live together but at
times I feel so lonely
I don't want to keep complaining, I
just want you on me or just hold me
I need more intimacy
you taking me for granted, Baby
and it hurts to think that maybe you're
just not into this lady

I want you to make a better effort in
making this a happy home
I'm tired of being alone
Tell me, what's going on?

# THE ANGRY WIFE

Happiness is whatever the fuck
I say it is
It damn sure aint living miserably
just for our kids
Nigga please, happiness is
finally realizing what YOU can and
cannot stand for
or better yet what YOU can deal with
Happiness is finally keeping it real
shit
Its saying, "who the fuck are you, to
tell me what should make me happy?"
when you're not the one living with
my baby daddy
I'm sorry my HUSBAND
don't know how to love me,
I'm having a hard time figuring out
just what it is he really wants this to
be
got me wondering, why did he even
marry me

Feels more like an agreement than a
commitment
at home, work, or with me and the
kids, is where his time should be
spent
except I'm left alone trying to
represent
a broken home
when we should have it going on
loving should be strong
but its weak like knees, got me over
here feeling like, nigga please
When is he gone try to make me
happy
he thinks being a provider is all he has
to be
that's just one part, what about being
a provider to me
Provide some spice, we need romance
in our life
hell I just wanna feel your touch at
night
I've given up on an active sex life
now that shit just aint right
no it aint all bad, but it could be a
whole lot better

don't deny that you don't even try,
you act like, its whatever
Instead of doing whatever it takes to
enlighten me
you seem content with me being
The Angry Wifey...

# STRANGE

Okay, what you call getting
yourself a little strange
was really a fucked up thing
You see, you didn't just cheat on me,
you cheated you
and for the record, I don't eat coochie
nigga, you do
You done stepped out there and got
you some strange
then tip-toe back home, acting like
shit aint changed
knowing I enjoy doing-the-damn-
thang
but I don't like sharing my ding-a-
lang
or having visions of your horrid sex
episodes
getting all freaky and tricking with
some Bitch,
breaking routine, thinking Shai
wouldn't know
Haven't you heard of women intuition
Bro?

Why?
Did I give you any reason to? Have I
ever denied you?
If there is a problem, bring it to the
table please
whatever is missing, let me satisfy
that need
Instead of keeping it real with her,
keep it real with me
If I'm not there for you or give you
more
then I could understand what you
cheating for
But you broke trust for lust and I
think it's so sick
why you would choose another
woman when I was yo first-pick.
Damn shame, all that's lost, behind
some damn strange…

# MY CHEATING HEART

Why do we have to be restricted
to dreams?
Why do we have to love without
being seen?
Why does it hurt facing what our
reality brings?
We could never be
my life belongs to someone else
and your heart isn't always with me
We share only a part of each other
that same part of me wants us to go
further
But where??
To a broken promise of being forever
mine
even if it's just for precious moments
in time
All I need to know is, in another
lifetime
could you, would you be all mines?

Not sharing, like we've been reduced
to do
would I be woman enough for you??
We've made a connection in such a
short period
got-a-sista trippin' like, "Is this
young brother serious?"
I sure do hope so
otherwise don't wake me I'm not
ready to let go
I'm needing to finish what we start
so please forgive
My Cheating Heart…

# CONFESSIONS

Can I confess to you on some real shit
on some, nigga can you really deal
wit it
I'm needing to keep it real, it's just
how I feel, shit

Can I confess to you that I make love
to you
and I'm fucking him too
but I'm not in love with you
aw don't front nigga, I been said what
I needed from you
and what you refused to
dis nigga now do
and trust, I'm no longer mad Boo

Can I confess to you that I want to be
alone
but still have you at home
and do what the fuck I want to, cause
shit I grown

and if we still wanna get-it-on
let's bone
just don't bring no bitches to our
home
and always answer yo cell phone
cause we still got kids so let's always
take care of home
and muthafuck what dem nigga's on
dis how WE do
I just wanna be happy,
nigga don't you?

KENERLY PRESENTS
LASHAI WOOD

# HOW MANY TIMES

How many times have I cried, can
you honestly say you tried
How many times have my requests
been denied?
How many times was I left home
alone?
and when I call yo phone you sound
like, "bitch leave me alone
stop sweating me, I'll be home"
How many times have you taken the
time to make sure my needs are met
How many times have I been
complaining and you haven't done
nothing yet
How many times have I told you I
was feeling lonely?
and that when we have sex is the only
time you really kiss or hold me
and it's not like we're sexually active,
which is a tragedy
I aint never known a nigga that don't

beat-up his in house pussy
and it not like we're shacking up,
nigga I'm yo wifey
How many times have I desired to be
your lover and not your hommie?
and not have to wait weeks for you to
bone me
I really don't think it's fair
that I hurt alone while you act like
you don't care
but when your feelings got hurt, you
went running scared
You filed for a divorce, when I
thought that wasn't a choice
or even an option, otherwise I would
have been on the first thing hopping
into court, hell, I could have filed for
divorce
But you call yourself a man,
punking-out when shit hit the fan
I'm sorry I reached out to another
man, but I felt like you tide my hands
but not once did I ever stop meeting
our homes demands
But what I cram to understand

is how you gon let a fuck come
between our love?
Really nigga, wassup?
Keep it real please
and "the fuck" I'm talking bout, is
you not giving a fuck about me…

# DON'T WALK AWAY

You can hate me for as long as it
takes, but please
DON'T WALK AWAY
I admit to all my mistakes but please
DON'T WALK AWAY
My debt I'll repay just
DON'T WALK AWAY.
Regardless of what we are feeling,
the healing
lies within the vows we made,
if I/we lose you forever, my heart
will break
I'm willing to do whatever it takes
to even the score, I just wanna know
that I'm worth fighting for,
you are, just
DON'T WALK AWAY
The past can't be erased
and what you're feeling now, is just a
phase
what happens when you realize that

this can't be replaced?
I'm begging you please
DON'T WALK AWAY
I'm learning my role, understanding I
must do as I'm told
I promised to have and to hold
our family is not worth letting go
and anything worth having, is worth
fighting for
I'm just wondering where is your
sword
Somewhere we forgot to care for one
another,
we stopped being husband and wife,
friends, and lovers
I'm sorry I reached out to another
JUST DON'T WALK AWAY

We both have been hurting for so long
and that can't be denied
but I'm here to tell you, that the grass
aint greener on the other side It's just
the DEVIL'S TRAP and I can't
apologize enough
please forgive me I know it's gon be
rough

but I just want US back
let's try to get the wisdom we lack, to
help keep us on track
cause I still love you and nothing will
ever change that
our kids living without their Dad at
home is wack
Every day I have to see the hurt in
their eyes
and I hate that you get to turn your
back
tears I have to fight back
I've cried alone enough already
and yes I know this burden is heavy
but HE promised not to put no more
on us than we can bare, nobody said it
would be easy and life can be unfair
but our lives feel empty without you
here
It's not about wrong or right
so why continue to question, argue,
fuss and fight
It's not about YOU or all about SHAI
it has everything to do with the three
kids we have to raise
we have corrections to make

that's when the healing takes place
So take all the time you need but all I
can say
is please, baby, baby, please
DON'T WALK AWAY...

# LISTEN

We've been married for years
now and we are more like roommates
afraid to communicate,
who barely date, nor do we participate
in a normal sex life
You treated me better and deserved
the pussy more
before I became your wife
Our firstborn, our only son is fifteen
years old
and let the truth be told
*NIGGA,* you use to caterer to my
every need
you never let our differences or
arguments get the best of *WE*
even when you pissed me off, you
never intentionally shitted on me
So now, how could I let this be
allow this same man to say he don't
know how to be good to me
when good is all he's ever been
I liked our relationship better when
we were parenting-friends

LASHAI WOOD

And *YES* I'll be the first to confess,
that I made a bigger mess
and that I'm blessed to still have you
by my side
even if you haven't or can't forgive
me, then why lie
why live an unfulfilling life
when it has always been up to *US* to
determine what's right
Feels like a game I didn't know we
was still playing
and all I'm saying
is let me know the rules, if the game
is still on, I wanna play too
I just wish I excited you like
drinking and smoking, kicking it, or
watching football do
you hate to miss or be late to things
that doesn't benefit *US* at all
Especially at a time like this, you're
more passionate about other bullshit
while I'm stuck wondering what part
of the game is this
when is the last time our tongues
kissed
like I said before, two can play, just

let me know the rules and shit
I pled guilty while you continue to
plead the fifth, too prideful to admit
your part in any of this shit
You says it was all my fault, that what
we had, we lost
and it's even harder to rebuild
I'm just wondering what happen to
the meaning of the word FORGIVE
because why did you really come
back home, for the kids?
That would be cool too
that's a lot better than walking out on
your family that needs you
and if that is the case, say it to my
face
it would make room for true healing
to take place
I've learned what true love is
Its understanding, its patient, its kind,
it's not demanding
Its saying I love you enough to not
hurt you anymore
It's being woman or man enough to
except that I still love you
but we're not *IN LOVE* anymore

LASHAI WOOD

It's willing to give you what you
deserve and need
its closing my eyes and allowing our
hearts to beat
even if we're not vibin' to the same
groove
its accepting I'm something like
R&B and you're more like old-school
It's accepting the things you cannot
change
its waiting for you to realize the same
thang
Its saying the things that need to be
said
its demanding your presences inside
my heart more than in our bed
Its requesting you to say just what
the fuck it is you really want from me
and how you really feel
it's getting you to see there's no
reason to kill at will
and please let's not forget that the
truth heals, so what's the deal?
Can you search your heart and keep
it real?

# SILLY

Silly of me to lose focus on what's
right
even if that nigga go to the left, stay
right
Silly of me to mistake good loving for
love
when the best loving comes from
above
Knowing I got work to do
while I can't move
I got moves to make, I got stuff to
prove
Got to prove that I can't lose
with God by my side I can't lose
not even if I wanted to
His Hands control all that I do
Silly that he don't know that too…

# GOODNITE NOT GOODBYE

It's not GOODBYE, it just
GOODNITE,
destiny means when the time is right
Love me enough to let me go,
what's meant to be, time will expose
if we don't stop now,
we'll never know
Sweet memories to have and to hold
is it true love
just SEARCH YO SOUL….
You are the answer to my
prayers, my me a' moiré
freely giving yourself
your heart, your body, your mind and
so much more
I don't deserve such a KING
something I thought was silly
turned out to be the man of my
dreams
how sad to face what our reality
brings

74

now is not our time
I'm married with children with my
life on the line
a person like you is so hard to find
the bond we share will always be
yours and mine
I believe we didn't meet and fall in
love by accident
I can't give up on the precious time
we spent
instead I ask for you to give me
space to let time erase
some of my mistakes
and when the smoke clears
then we can deal with our fears
We can be together as one, at the
right time
and in the same place
we will define the expression of
"soul mates"
Our hearts will reunite and our souls
will intertwine
it's not fair, I have all of yours and
you get only half of mines
it should be yours all the time and
since that can't be

Badu, Badu, I guess I'll see you next
lifetime.
GOODBYE is forever, GOODNITE
is until we meet again
LOVE is forever and so is being
friends
It's not GOODBYE, it's just
GOODNITE
destiny means when the time is right
Love me enough to let me go
what's meant to be, time will expose
Sweet memories, to have and to hold,
is it true love SEARCH YO SOUL....

# SIGNS

Talking bout signs,
they are all around you, so don't be
blind
You gotta stop speeding,
slow down
it's not about what you've been
needing
HE is alive
got pulled over for doing 60 in a 45
Didn't you see the overpass?
watch out, you're going nowhere fast
knowing you should stop but yo
heavy foot is on the gas
passing up signs
sacrificing the PROMISE that's
yours and mines
Messing up and living all stressed
forgetting that you are blessed
how could you be so pressed or settle
for anything less
because the devil is a mess
thinking you wouldn't pass the test
doubting that the vision will ever

manifest
when all you need to do is confess
and HIS grace guarantees success
you could never be cripple if you
walk with JESUS
You cannot be moved
and if you need it in writing, the
Bible is your tool
We were made in HIS image and the
power is inside of you
so don't be blind
lean not unto thy own understanding,
just look at the signs…

# WITH YOU

When we first started messing around
you said you didn't mind
sharing time
I soon fell in love with the ideal that
your body was all mine
now feelings have crossed the line
you want my loving all the time
and when we fuck you whisper,
"This pussy is mine"
excuses to leave home is getting hard
to find
and let you tell it, now your heart is
on the line
when before our arrangement was just
fine
I was yours to enjoy only when I had
the time
Now the game has transformed like
Optimist Prime
and this situation is blowing my mind
with ultimatums keeping me confined
Lost in thoughts of,
"what-the-fuck should I do"

yes I'm married but I'm falling for
another dude
don't judge and say, "How dare you?"
when neglect, disrespect, and take me
for granted, is what my husband do
I know, "why not leave?" I been
wanting to
but it's not just about me, we got kids
too
so to keep slippin and trippin on my
hubby is what I won't do
I'll just creep with boyfriend number
two
There's no need to wonder if what I
feel is true
otherwise I couldn't have given my
loving to someone new
No I'm no longer confused
home is not that bad now that I can
have my cake and eat it too
No it's not what I really want but for
now it will do
I enjoy just being WITH YOU

# ONE OR THE OTHER

First, let me mention, I was a married
women who had no intentions
of cheating
but somehow I found myself torn
between what feels good and what's
right
ONE could be the best blessing if
only he'd run toward the light
THE OTHER is just some act right
ONE is a supposed to, something I
gotta do
THE OTHER is something I wanna
do
ONE is stuck in his old ways
THE OTHER is all about pleasing
Shai
I feel like ONE is just with me for the
kids and the convenience
and he's something like stingy with
his penis
THE OTHER just wants to see me

happy and enjoy spoiling my entire
body
tries very hard to make the most of
the time spent with me
So I'm stuck between a rock and a
hard place
Needing the ONE to save face
while THE OTHER will do whatever
it takes and haven't stopped yet
it would be easier to believe if I said it
was all about the sex
but what THE OTHER offers is more
intimate
he gives me true companionship

ONE or THE OTHER could have
been the best
but ONE refused to study and THE
OTHER passed the test…

# DO IT AGAIN

After months of separation,
my body was anticipating
the feel of his touch
couldn't pick him up from the bus
station fast enough
In the p.m. at 11:35 he hoped in my
ride
kissing me desperately, before I could
even put the truck in drive
We headed straight for the Marriott
but we didn't check right in
he just had to have me right then
In the back of the hotel parking lot,
my panties dropped
and to the back seat we hopped, he
dove right in like a pig on slop
after my love came cumming down,
he climbed on top
then he gave me the business, pulling
my hair asking,
"Whose pussy is this?"
I'm moaning, "Yours, yours"
he rolled me over and gave me more,

more
We switched positions, we missed
tasting each other's kissing
plus my knee was hitting the seat belt
and he was ready for me to ride him if
nothing else
We had the best I-miss-you-sex
it was so intense, so passionate
It got so steamy and hot that we
fogged up the windows
went at it for as long as who knows
Finished-up, zipped-up, then we
checked right in
we needed more room so we could
DO IT AGAIN…

# BUST-A-MOVE

After our group date, we quietly
escaped
To our private section, my body
needed flexin
he was my Mystikal and I was his
video vixen
I wanted to give him some of my love
and affection
make love till our skins become one
complexion
I wanted to thank him for just loving
me
for stopping my broken hearts bleed
for clearing the air so that my lungs
could breath

Earlier, we enjoyed our friends and
barbeque grilled to perfection
now it was time for my favorite
dessert, sex with no protection
Making love to Ricky Ross
In my ear he's whispering, "I'm the

biggest boss"
In his rhythm I gets lost
all his hip-hop gets me off
He put it down and as nasty as it may
sound
I savored his dick dog when my knees
hit the ground
but hold the special sauce, my coochie
was hungry and jealous too
it said, "You suck the bone, just save
me the juice"
Not to mention he wants to reproduce
I would just love to have his lil'
Shorty too
but for right now, Imma just enjoy my
Young MC bust-a-move

# LOVE IS GREAT

I went from blowing the horn at the
window for him to let me in
or barely coming to visit him
from being a nobody, to becoming his
hommie-lover-friend
I went from using a spare key
to special Cleveland Browns one
made just for me
And I swear this love is great
I went from escaping home to us
sharing his place
got me a lil nigga willing to do
whatever it takes
to put a smile on my face
he puts dinner on my plate
forgives my mistakes
not to mention the sex is great
In the bed he does whatever it takes
to put a smile on my face
I put my dinner on his plate
leaves a mess on his face
In his dessert I partake

87

we share dreams of being in a better
place
committed to doing whatever it takes
proving to each other that being in
Love is Great…

KENERLY PRESENTS
LASHAI WOOD

# A PLACE I CALL HOME

Let me tell yall bout HOME
cause as soon as you stick that
Cleveland Brown key in the lock,
it's on
I feel right at home
In the living room is where we camp
out playing games
we entertain, drinking, and smoking
on dem thangs
We listen to music or watch TV
the queen size mattress from the
bedroom is where he groove me
In the kitchen, dis nigga be mixing
and cooking up three square meals
no box recipes, no shortcuts,
I'm talking real
Real herbs and spices fixing
homemade gravy
heart-shaped or Mickey Mouse
pancakes made just for me
Not to mention, the rosemary chicken

with sides and dessert cooked to
perfection
Dinner with Musiq, wine, and
candlelight
in the bedroom its whatever I like
Not really a dining room more like an
area just for two
a small bar with matching bar stools
In the bathroom, is where we assume
the position
washing where our hands be missing
kissing, slipping and sliding, and
lathering up with the soap suds
steamed filled room, Musiq still
bumpin, now dats what's up
Using the water dripping for four-play
then he bends me over and wax that
bootay
Wash and rinse again, dry off, and
then we brush our teeth
turn off the lights then hit dem sheets
In the bedroom, is where I go voom-
voom and shake my rump
we get crump in here like Akon and
Lil' John
ecstasy is where he takes me all night

long
like Lionel Richie, we gets busy
Show me what you working wit, then
we lick, lick, licky, lick
Yes I let him lick da wrapper
then shorty get her nut, smack me on
da butt
Mama like to fuck, you know I like it
ruff, one nut is not enough
Okay, now after you pick it up and
stop, we drop
off into a deep sleep, snuggled up
close using bodies for heat
Behind closed doors we have it going
on
in our one bedroom apartment BIG
enough to call home…

# HOME

I wanna go home
to a place where I belong
loving and living with my man and
my kids
with no regrets, forgiven for things I
did
Lord, I know what YOU can do
so please, do
I'm confused and feel abused
A skilled worker with no tools,
feet too big for these shoes
I feel beat-up and broke down
but how could that be, when my
FATHER wears a crown
and has the power to turn any
situation around
Jesus please, turn now
Cause I've had enough of this detour
and I can't take much more
tears falling out of control and my
eyes are sore
seriously, Lord, I can't take much
more

Wondering what are YOU waiting for
I heard YOUR knock, I answered the
door
Come into my house and bless my
home
quiet this storm
I'm ready to take on a new form
define why I was born
PLEASE FATHER, I'M TIRED OF
FEELING TORN

KENERLY PRESENTS
LASHAI WOOD

# IT SHOULDN'T MATTER

IT SHOULDN'T MATTER
as long as he makes me smile
who cares that you think our
possibilities are only for a little while
To feel like this
is something I don't wanna miss
　　IT SHOULDN'T MATTER
that he is young
as long as, he knows where I'm
coming from
romantically serious but we still have
fun
　　IT SHOULDN'T MATTER
that he's not "THERE"
as long as he's going somewhere
have dreams of taking me there
now or never, who cares?
and if or when it happens, at least I
can say, "I was there"
　　IT SHOULDN'T MATTER
as silly as it may seem

as long as I found the man of my
dreams
He's like dope and I'm like a fiend
we're like biggest fans cheering for
the same team
    IT SHOULDN'T MATTER
that yall still like my ex-husband, hell,
I do to
but things didn't go as planned, I've
accepted it, so why can't you
we're better friends and parents and
that's just cool
as long as when it comes to our kids,
we make it do what it do
I can't lie, I enjoyed the ride
but when the excitement is over, I
stop being afraid to say bye-bye

    IT SHOULDN'T MATTER,
    AT LEAST I TRIED

# NOW HEAR THIS!!

*You wanted a relationship poem,
well this is more like an exhale
because I only wanna say this
once and then I'm gonna exhale*

Unanswered cell phones, accepting
collect prison calls
from cripples that CAN walk
excuses and emotional abuses
drug addicts with bad habits
has-beens, straight-up losers who
can't win
treating them all better than kin
Catering to these men
and mad that I've found a friend, who
comprehends
the pursuit of happiness
Whatever happen to minding yo
business?
I don't know what it is for you and I
aint mad I must say

but for ME, this describes my happy
day;
I wake up to Mickey Mouse or heart-
shaped pancakes, sausage fried to
perfection, and eggs with cheese
I aint got no reason to lie, nigga
please
Baby I miss you and when you
coming home phone calls throughout
the day
flowers when he can and cards to say
what he feels, all cause he loves to see
the pretty smile of Shai
I get a hot meal seasoned to kill
we hold hands, say grace, and smash
the food on our plates
but because I don't have to cook, I do
the dishes, but I don't mind
cause I've learned to clean-up behind
myself, when I use to cook
oh I'm not finish, come take a closer
look
I get cuddled on all day long
I lay with a man that bumps gansta
rap but make love to slow songs
I snuggle with a dude that loves to rub

and touch
he's something like a M&M, soft in
the middle but hard with a crunch
He got a pretty smile, good-ass hair,
he cute, and he can sang
Let's not talk about the sex, let's just
say he can do-the-damn-thang
twelve inches and some change, and
is willing to do anything
to please thee
may not be enough for you, but it's
alright wit me
Cause if I'm gon struggle, and we all
do
I don't mind going through the storm
with a lover so true
But what I can't understand for the
life of me
is, I'm not mad at you, so why not
just let us be?
You get so tired of pleading your case
and trying to get a person to
understand you
but if you really think about it, what
do "they" matter, they can't define
your happiness, you have to

and people gon always talk about you,
but they really mad Boo
Wishing they could be you or walk in
yo shoes
instead they lie and make-up thangs, I
know, I've done it too
exaggerate, but now I don't have to
All that I need he gives and what he
don't have, he tries to
I don't like sharing, nor do I have to
Look but don't touch I suggest you
get yo own Boo…

# FEEL SO GOOD

Baby feel so good 2 me
Fingertips, sumthing like shocks me
tingling my entire body
Don't worry, I'll wait
don't wanna escape
a feeling like this
made loved 2 and kissed
with my hair tangled in his fist
pulling while he's hittin dis

Yeah, baby feel so good 2 me
defines the word ecstasy
in every which-a-way he can
but loose
together we produce
perfect harmony
his groove got me singing softly
his warm body I don't want off me
until he gets me off or turn dat ass
around
smack-it-up flip-it, then rub it down

Um, baby, baby, baby feel so damn

good 2 me
tongue kissing my soul
inside I explode
Now my mouth wants to know
how does it feel
in and out then back down south
but this time, just put it in my mouth
Yeah, baby feel so good 2 me…..

# I LIKE

I like his dick
the way it fit's
the way he be rubbin' his shit
I like his kiss
the way he licks and stick
his tongue in me
suck so passionately
I like his hands on my hips
squeezing and pinching my titts
while he French kiss my clit
keeps me cumming and shit
sheets wetter than a bitch
pussy farting and shit
I like his smile and the sound of his
laugh
I like the circumference of his
cylinder yall do the math
I like the feel of the biggest dick I
ever had
I like the way we rub face and the
way he taste
and our dreams of being in another
place

I like his eyes searching my soul
and him schooling me on the things I
don't know
Yeah, I like dis lil nigga for sho…

KENERLY PRESENTS

LASHAI WOOD

# RAPPER'S DELIGHT

I just gotta have dat JEZZY
to please me
cause my shit gets hot n greasy like
WAKA FLOCKA FLAME
I'm in love with me some good
dang-a-lang
as long as it aint no LIL' WAYNE
I'm looking for a little more than just
TWO-CHAINZ
A sista is looking for dat FUTURE in
her life
who can BUSTA RHYME and
XHIBIT all night
go Ludicris when he laying pipe
So I hope you 2Pacn' dat BIGGIE cuz
Imma need some RICKY ROSS
to get me off, shit in that bedroom
bitch I'm a boss
Oooweee some T.I.P
I'll give and take some of dat gladly
cause I keeps my DOUGIE FRESH

I only got one protest
and no I'm not sad to say
you can't get none of this KANYE
so so sorry I don't swing dat way
that end is for exits only
And all I'm taking from-da-back
is some SNOOP DOGGY DOG cause
I love dat
To da sack
you can bring whatever you need
some ICE CUBE, dat FAT JOE and
some DR. DRE chronic weed
just as long as my GUCCI get what
she need
I really don't care if it's wrong or right
just lay dat pipe
for my RAPPER'S DELIGHT

# THIS OR THAT

I'm looking for a man who got my
back
Whatever I want and need he should
take care of that
and if he aint got-it, he should say
some shit like, "Shai I be right back
let me go get dat"
All his love, respect, and trust he
should gimmie that
give it to me and I give it right back
When he open his mouth, he should
speak nothing but fact
the truth hell we both deserve dat
I'm looking for a man with a life and
game plan on da map
with good direction and all of dat
A family guy with a sense a humor on
top of that
but bullshit he don't give or take none
of dat
and if my nigga fall down, my nigga
bounce back

LASHAI WOOD

he should hustle hard flip and stack
dat
so what's in his wallet, he can gimmie
that
He gone throw me like he know me,
or keep moving black
Because see I need a man who gone
kiss my dis and my dat
only this ass he tap
give-it-to-me real good from the back
pulling my hair so we can kiss, he
know I love dat
You see I couldn't be asking for too
much because I'm promised all of this
and all of that
So yall I'm looking for this nigga,
have you seen him?
Do you know where he at?
if you do, tell him holla and I holla
back
so he can give me
all of THIS and all of THAT

# DRINKS ON ME

Drinking so heavily
not even knowing that he
is killing me softly
two-timing me
and his infidelity began with this bad
ass brown bitch named Hennessey
said he met her at the club through his
cousin Remy
Then I caught um brown-bagging
Wild Irish Rose
getting tow, taking her down real slow
He hit her straight-up wit no chaser
his lips couldn't hardly wait to taste
her
had me at home on some,
"I see you later"
And it took Absolut-ly
took everything in me
to get over him and the twins
that damn Ciroc and Gin
yeah they did him dirty so we are no
longer lovers or friends
You see he just can't refuse

or turn loose no Goose
and if you coming up off dat Cuervo
he aint gone say no
bottoms up is how he roll
and swear he not cheating but I can
smell it under his nose
Thought I didn't notice when he
was eyeballing da lil freak Bacardi
wit his 151 excuses nigga please
knowing he popping bottles and
cherries
how dare he
but he swear he care for me
but I swear he don't protect my heart
carefully
drinking so heavily
not even knowing that he
is killing me softly
two-timing me
with a bitch he chose
at the gotdamn liquor sto

KENERLY PRESENTS

LASHAI WOOD

# PEACE

For the first time in thirty six months, peacefully asleep in the fetal position, there he lies, shirtless with his life story tatted across his belly, back, arms, and chest. With the capital letters "A-Z-I-K-I-W-E" engraved across his shoulder blades, from a nightmare he awakes.

Startled until he feels the warmth of her smooth dark skin and with a smile, he rolls over to the left to share another first kiss with his hearts one true love. He licks his dry lips and plants a good morning kiss on

her forehead, then her left eyelid and
left cheek.
Not trying to disturb her
beauty sleep or peace
just a small gesture to thank the
Lord for the blessing of her beauty,
her essence, her love, and endurance
to have faithfully stood by his side.
It can't be denied,
their undying love has
withstood all odds, breaking the age
difference barriers that has left the
world judging her so called
animalistic ways,
a cougar some might say.
It would shock that same world
to know that he was the one on the

prey.

Being fifteen years apart, she

was unsure from the start,

yet he took her broken heart,

her damaged goods, and put

his mending hands to work and

together, they produced something

damn good.

They shared similar interest and

honest truths

she was able to freely discuss

suffered neglect, emotional and verbal

abuse.

He quickly became her

shoulder and arms that she could go

running to

Instantly, she became the only

family he knew

in a strange city and the

woman's touch that he had long for so

much.

Often living on borrowed time,

long distance between them,

significant others, and obligations,

somehow an understanding, a desire,

and love developed into promises to

forever be true

and allow time to prove in

which direction the relationship

should move.

Just when things between them

were getting comfortable

off to prison he had to go.

Faced with three years, his

manhood would be established and
defined
and she would discovered that
it had been true love all this time
and that her stubbornness and
his thug-life mentality had robbed
them blind.  Or had her insecurities
and stupidity forced his hand into a
life of crime. He snaps backs to
reality, when she moans and cuddles
up next to him.  The heat from his
warm and caramel complexion feels
like paraffin wax sticking to her body
as he climbs on top of her voluptuous
dark chocolate frame.  Last night
could never be enough to satisfy his
undying thirst for her passion fruit

after having gone without her for so

long, it had almost killed him, but the

thought of drinking from her nectar,

gave him the

strength to survive.

Her body was full of sleeping

desires and requires spontaneous

combustion that boils inside of only

him.

Faking sleep because she

secretly loves when their eyes first

meet awaken by his good morning

pleasures.  Moaning and whispering

as he enters her real deep and grinding

slow,

caressing her tightly,

never wanting to let go,

no longer concerned if she is
asleep anymore.

Their bodies were both
wanting, needing to reunite as one,
and fulfill the once denied ability to
satisfy each other or even cry in the
arms of one another.

For what seemed like an
eternity, for hours, they were able to
reassure each other's broken sprits,
reconnect and consummate their unity
of finally becoming husband
and wife.

After a six year courtship, the
roller coaster ride, the breaking of
some family ties,
the acceptance of mistakes,

hidden truths and lies,

together hand and hand, their

spiritual bond was tied.

Aggressively thrusting to leave

all the pain and suffering endured

behind.

engulfed in sweat and tears the

Presley's made love for what seemed

like the very first time

Resting In Peace

**BETWEEN THE SHEETS**

# I MISS YOU

I miss yo morning breath
complimented by good morning sex

and them goofy lil "I miss you" text

or calling just to remind me that last
night was the BEST

I miss eating and sleeping with you

and the way our bodies groove

I miss yo hands touching all ova my
body

and the way you bite yo bottom lip
when it's time to get naughty

I miss yo good looking and yo damn
good cooking

I miss the taste of you


Yo lips, yo manliness

yo tongue, yo fingertips

I MISS YOU

Yo touch

yo hands on my neck or pulling my
hair or spreading my thighs

my soul misses your searching eyes

I miss yo chest to fall asleep and yo
reassurance of peace

I miss my Mr. All I Need

I MISS YOU

# U MIGHT BE BUT IT STILL AIN'T ME

Yall chicks can't roll like me

can't go like me

don't hang like me

can't bang like me

can't blow dem thangs like me

don't think like me

can't bank like me

won't bump like me

shake rump like me

aint go stunt like me

no packs like me

can't stack like me

aint got muscle like me

cant hustle like me

aint dope like me

don't got flow like me

can't let go like me

I AM THE S-H-I-T so you can't be funkier than ME

# WHY I CHOSE TO LOVE

Yes I really enjoyed being his friend

but his unconditional loving made me
want him for my man

His compromise opened my eyes

and my heart was exposed as he
accepted my truths n lies

he held me in his arms as I cried

then took me to church and let me
testify

He is GOD fearing with a love that is
never ending

with him there's no pretending

I can just be me

and even when I don't feel like it, he
stay in love with me

infatuated with my dirty draws

rather they fat or small

hair combed or not at all

loving me when I'm up but even more
when I fall

How others think about us, to him it
really don't matter at all

and when it comes to love-making he
has a freaky protocol

and he stay true to his motto

STAY LOYAL AND LOVE LIKE
THERE IS NO TOMORROW

# MY DAD SAY

I was something like a crip as a runt

a lil black Forrest Gump

Born with bowlegs times three

so my mother chose to correct my feet

"Early my legs were broke" and put
into cast then I sported them
corrective shoes

the ones with a bar in between them
connecting the two

All that I went through before the age
of two

so I don't really know when I really
started walking to tell you the truth

But when I took my first steps,

I stepped off and got lost

Riding dirty with my Daddy in the
fast lane

witnessing him get into all kinds of
gangsta thangs

He taught me how to switch lanes and
maintain my cool

cheat if I must but never let the right
hand know what the left one do

Trust only when its earned and giving
back to you

and do whatever it takes just to make
it through

no matter how hard it get,

By Any Means Necessary Boo

I still can hear his words, I live by and
hold them true

There will NEVER be another like
my Daddy, Herbert Hasan Lee

and if you thought you was hard
nigga, he would take it to the street

Might not been shit to them others be
he was alright with me

# SISTA 2 SISTA

She got me ova here feeling like

Carl Thomas,

"wishing I neva met her at all even
though I love her so"

But oh well

say she love me, shit I can't tell

It's all good when it's all going well

but one misunderstanding and she
already to bail

She don't just run but she push a sista
away

with tough love, abusive thoughts and
words that I could never even think to
say

Then got the nerve to call me fake

when what I mean I do and say

and if I got a problem, I wanna Talk
about it that day

talk to yo face

fix n get equipped for the next
challenge that comes my way

But regardless of how heartless she
ACT, I choose to love her anyway

Unlike she, I can accept the
differences between we

and understand that we LOVE
different, because we were LOVED
differently

# CASH OVA EVERYTHANG

Tick tock

goes the sound of my biological clock

something I can't stop

so here I go, to my knees I drop

as my head go tick tock on my
YOUNG JOCK

tongue like zoom zoom zoom

we in the bedroom

and all I want is some YOUNG
BUCK

said all he had was FIFTY CENT

hand out shaking my damn head
cause he got me bent

I need a CASH MONEY  brotha to
keep my MANNIE FRESH

don't play me cheesy cause my
WEEZY F. BABY is the best

Understand that I need more than a
BIRD MAN

to stop the itching in my right hand

I need a man to help me fly right

keep my GAME and B.G. tight

TURK and tweak my JUVENILE
ways

so that I can express my Shades of
Shai

still I don't want nobody's spare
change

cause IT'S CASH OVA
EVERYTHANG

# LOVE DON'T COST A THING

How can one believe in LOVE if they
aint never seen

don't know a gotdamn thing

only experienced LOVE watching a
movie or in a dream

but never felt the real thing

While women settle for a Martin
Luther without the KING

forgetting that gotdamnit  we queens

LOVE shouldn't be one-sided

it should feel equally divided

real LOVERS don't want to hide it

they fight just to lay beside it

We both can have everything

just tell me what song you like

and baby I will sing

just don't play with my emotions
cause LOVE DON'T COST A
THING

# WHENEVER I WANT 2

I traveled what seemed like a million miles away

just 2 see his face and embellish in our tongues taste

Memorized by his eyes and how his hustle hand always supplies

fighting back tears I silently cry

because after years of hiding denying and lying we still can't be

just when I was feeling free

to love, my nigga got locked up

At a time in my life when I don't just want anything

I desire something real, a certain thing

The comfort of knowing that he love
me more than enough for the two

got my body so spoiled nothing else
will ever do

they may pay or pacify me but
nothing else quite FEEL like my dude

And not to be rude

but folk just don't know how good
they got it too

being able to kiss hug touch laugh and
fuck whenever they want to

taking days and life for granted
walking round with attitudes

Man damn they just don't know what I
wouldn't do

to kiss this nigga whenever I wanted
to.

# IT'S LIKE CANDY

Sex to me, is like biting into a

York Peppermint Patty

I get the HOT sensation of penetration
with no hesitation

our steamy love-making be creating
such passion

got my nigga asking,

"Whose pussy is" this?

as he fills me up with his
circumference

Before we even begin even before
entering

I'm hot, wet, and tingling

about the thought of our brown skins
intertwining

Don't get it twisted, the best sex is not
the BIGGEST dick

it's about ALL the work you put into
it

and if size is not your 4tay

then develop yo skills in foreplay

and get it popping that way

SO THAT THE NEXT TIME U
TAKE A BITE INTO DAT CANDY

ENJOY IT LIKE IT WAS YO LAST
DAYS

# I'M HUNGRY

I'm a starving artist famine for this
shit

a lil big boned, not greedy,

but I'm a hungry bitch

Born ready to fix then lick what's left
off da plate

go back for seconds and then say my
grace

My gluttony forces me

to eat up everything in front of me

and lyrically I'm stuffed so I cannot
breathe

belly on swollen, can't see my feet

the Fat Boys and got shit on me

open up all night All I Can Eat

appetite so big, buffet can't feed me

when I walk in the door you can tell
I'M HUNGRY

# SMDH

Why is it so hard to talk to the one
you love

Where is the understanding,

where's the love

Instead of listening we battle for the
mic

free styling about who is wrong or
who is right

I just can't understand why a person
would wanna be upset for days

but prides punks us out of saying what
we need to say

or even changing our ways

In order to feel better you should
wanna heal together

whether the storms of any weather

Instead one sleeps in bitter peace
while the other weeps

both suffering from the agony of
defeat

You should want to apologize to stop
the crying eyes

otherwise how can u even say you
tried

You should wanna give your all when
you can

or except when your are left alone and
feel abandon...

SMDH....

# PUFF PUFF PASS IT

Let me break it down in layman so
you can understand my need

WEED is dat glass of wine dat bubble
bath

dat rush you get from buying some
new shoes or Gucci Bag

Its dat mood stabilizer

its dat, I don't like it down here

I wanna go higher

Its dat fuck it, I just got fired

or dat it aint shit I can do, shit I'm
tired

its dat icebreaker

that even chill playa haters

Its legal in some states which I think
is great

it help those to self-medicate

it low-key ease the pain and it can
assist with weight gain

helps to maintain and endure the
strain

It helps you to stay sane

And all I know is, without it Ricky
Williams aint been the same

and from the first hit that you inhale,
you be on some, oh well

it is what it is

I be numb to it all wit just one spliff

and it can't be all that bad,

Mother Earth grows it

So aww shut up and just

PUFF PUFF PASS IT

# A LETTER FROM MY LOVE

11-5-2010  1:14 a.m.

Hey my IttyBitty,

I can't stand thoughts of losing you again

I will fight for you from within

and pray you can't live without my loving

Hope you still excited to finish what we began

On them bad days, think of it like I'm your soldier away at war

until the thought of being without US don't hurt no more

You are the love of my life

145

and we been through too much not to
stick it out and do things right

Besides I can't see myself with
nobody else

this time I don't wanna share,

I want you all to myself

I miss pulling yo hair and you yelling
out my name

I miss your kiss, your touch, your feel

you are my reason to live for real

I just can't wait to touch your body
and be tangled up with you in the bed

or hear your laughter about the jokes
that we said

Just when I got you use to the sex that
ONLY I CAN deliver,

it was taken away.

I promise it won't be long baby,

lil Daddy will be home real soon and don't worry I will fulfill your every fantasy

I be whatever you want and need.

This place has been a blessing and a curse

it has allowed us to grow even though the separation hurts

I'm a much better person, better for you and me,  better for us

and TRUST I aint going nowhere.  I messed up already and I feel like I let you down but I will make up for all of that.  I will be the best man I can be

I will try my hardest to make you happy and proud of me,

I owe you that much at least.

I have faith in my abilities, near or
far, I will tend to your needs

Can't nobody love you like me

and even when they try, they still aint
me.

In my darkest hour, you didn't give up
on me

you didn't leave and treated me like
yo king

when I was in the most pain, you were
there

and I thank God for sending me you

and I promise to forever stay loyal
and true

If nothing else be a man of my word
and invite you to share my world

for as long as you will have me.

Later I'm getting yo name tatted on
my left hand cause you have never
left me

and so I can kiss it, I miss you so
much.

I'm so glad and proud of you lil mama
making changes for the better

and I know it's been stormy weather

without me

but that too shall pass just hold on to
your faith

and pray for the wisdom to
understand just what God has in store
for us

I just pray we continue to grow closer.

I will forever trust you with my life,
soul, and heart and don't you worry
your pretty little head, you ARE ALL
I want

I just don't want to be played with, if
you can't handle this shit babe

I have no choice but to understand
just tell me first please.

I love you because I can't live without
you because you mean the world to
me

you are my everything.  Listen to me
sounding all Toni Braxtonish

NO HOMMO, U already know how
yo nigga roll lol.

But seriously babe, I need for you to
stay strong and please try not to cry

this will only make us stronger and
you know how I feel about you

Just smile for lil Daddy and fuck
anybody who on dat negative shit

we both know life is too short and
tomorrow is not promised

They should know by now that I ain't
going no where

and your heart don't want no one else
there.


I promise to never put you or myself
in this position ever again

I won't ever abandon my best friend

being away from you is killing me
and I thank God for you being in my
life

I love and miss you with all my might

So put on yo fuck um dress girl

and dance yo troubles away because I
love you with all my heart

I will never give up on trying to be the
man you want and need

because that man is all the man I want
to be....


I LOVE YOU THE MOST

Trust 1:1